Morgan Hill Country School
Holly Day Book Fair
1999

A gift

For   <u>The Library</u>

From<u>Book Fair Profit</u>

THE HUMAN MACHINE

THE
FOOD PROCESSOR

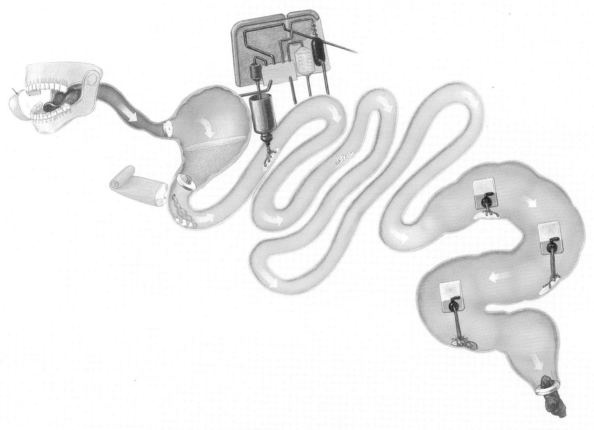

Sarah Angliss

Illustrations by Graham Rosewarne

Thameside Press

Distributed in the United States by
Smart Apple Media
123 South Broad Street
Mankato, Minnesota 56001

Text copyright © Sarah Angliss 1999

Editor: Susie Brooks
Designer: Helen James
Educational consultant: Carol Ballard

Printed in Singapore

ISBN 1-929298-17-X
Library of Congress Catalog Card Number 99-73403

10 9 8 7 6 5 4 3 2 1

Words in **bold** are explained in the glossary on pages 30 and 31.

CONTENTS

THE FOOD PROCESSOR

Think of your body as an amazing machine—a human machine. Think of your food as fuel that helps the machine to run. Your digestive system is a special food processor that breaks down food, absorbs the nutrients from it, and disposes of the useless waste.

Twisty tube

Food enters your body through your mouth. The waste products—**urine** and **feces**—come out the other end. Between the two ends there's a huge network, called your digestive system, that's built around one main tube.

Your digestive tube can be up to 30 feet long. It's bent and coiled in places so it fits inside your body. Food that travels along it is gradually broken down into chemical substances that your body can absorb and use.

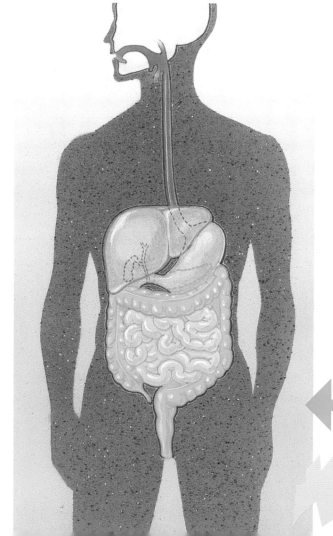

Look out for pictures like this one throughout the book. They show where each part of the digestive system is positioned in your body.

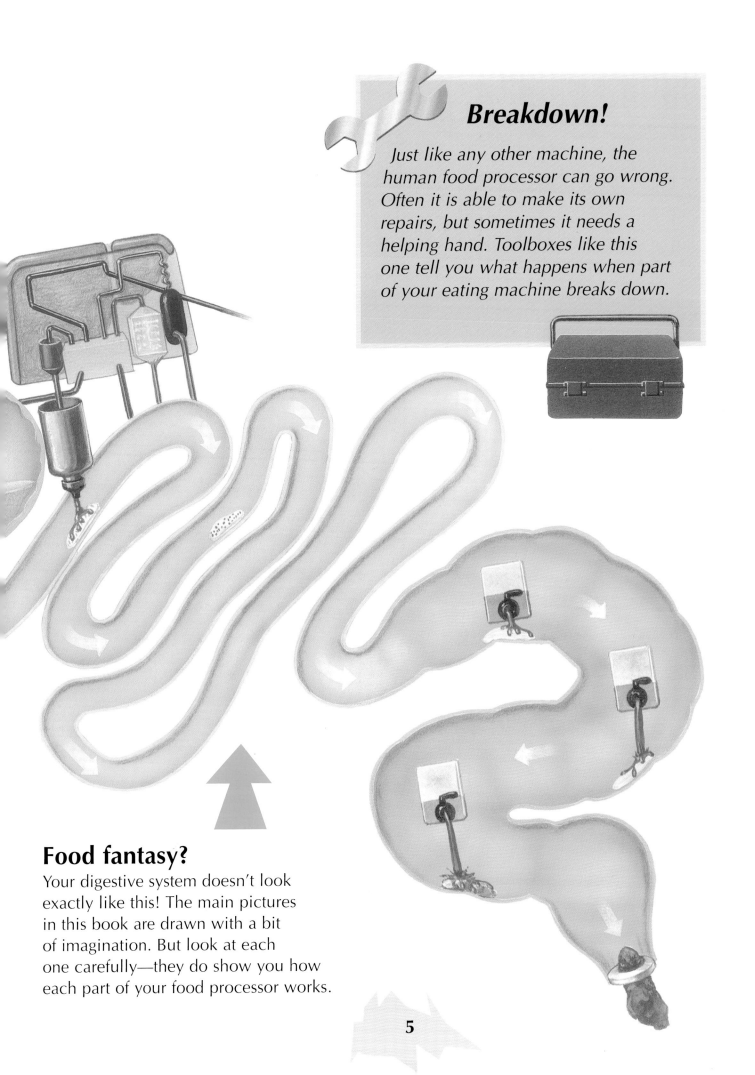

Food fantasy?

Your digestive system doesn't look exactly like this! The main pictures in this book are drawn with a bit of imagination. But look at each one carefully—they do show you how each part of your food processor works.

TEETH

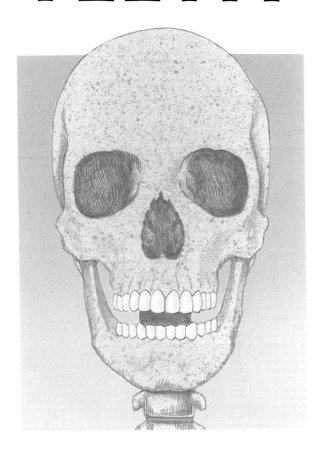

Most food comes in chunks that are too big to swallow whole. That's why the human machine has teeth to cut food into lumps, chop it up, and then grind it. Teeth come in lots of different shapes.

Chopping and chewing

The shape of each tooth suits a certain job. The **incisors** act as choppers. They are shaped like spades and can bite off lumps of food. **Canines** are the sharp, pointed teeth found on each side of the incisors. They are your shredders—they rip lumps of food into smaller pieces. Your **molars** are wide and flat to grind your food into a pulp.

Your teeth are squeezed and pushed a lot when you chew, so they have to be firmly fixed into your jaw. Each tooth has little bony prongs, called roots, to keep it in place. They fit inside holes in your jawbone. You can't see these prongs; they are hidden by your gums.

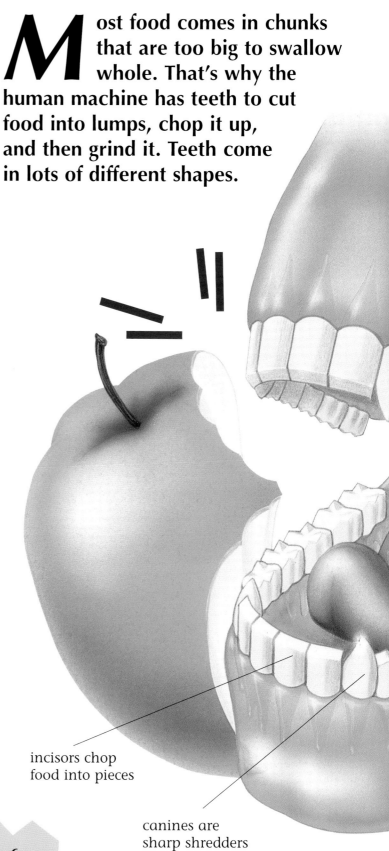

incisors chop food into pieces

canines are sharp shredders

6

Baby teeth

Adults can have up to 32 teeth. Young children's jaws are too tiny to hold that many, so they start off with about 20 baby teeth. From the age of five they begin to lose these and adult teeth grow instead.

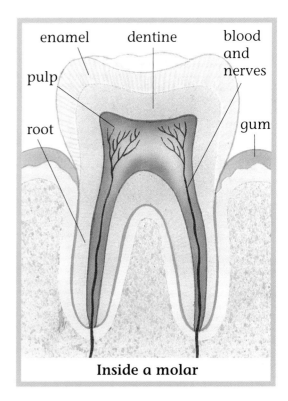

enamel   dentine   blood and nerves

pulp

root

gum

Inside a molar

What's inside?

Deep inside every tooth is a soft pulp, full of blood and **nerves** that help to keep it alive. On top of this is a bone-like layer called **dentine**. The pearly white coating on your teeth is called **enamel**, which is the hardest stuff in your whole body. It protects the layers underneath.

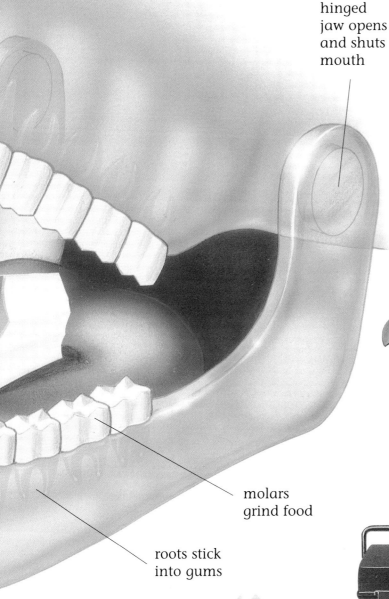

hinged jaw opens and shuts mouth

molars grind food

roots stick into gums

Crooked teeth

Teeth don't always grow in neat rows. If your teeth are very crooked, your dentist may suggest you wear braces. These are wire frames that go over your teeth and pull on them gently, aligning them so you end up with a nice straight smile.

JUICE MAKERS

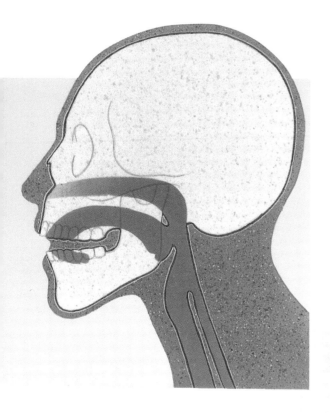

Every human machine has a mixing, mashing food sampler—your tongue—and lots of little juice makers called salivary glands. These work together to help move food around your mouth and turn it into soft, moist lumps.

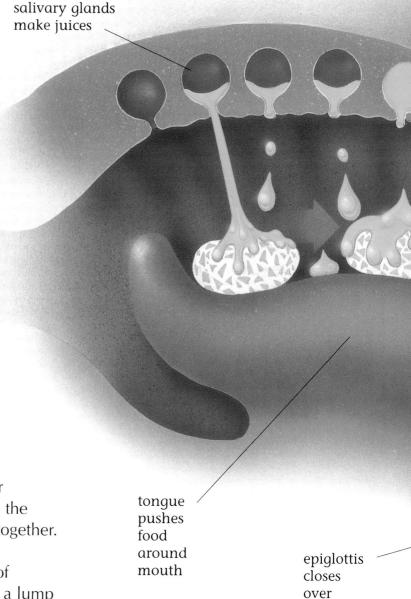

salivary glands make juices

tongue pushes food around mouth

epiglottis closes over windpipe

Munching to mush

Does your mouth water when you dream about your favorite foods? Although we call it "water," the real name for the juice inside your mouth is **saliva**. It's made in your salivary **glands**. The more you chew or think about food, the more juice is produced.

As you chew, your tongue moves food around your mouth, mixing it with your saliva. The saliva begins to break down the food, soften it up, and bind the pieces together.

Your tongue also presses against the roof of your mouth, squeezing the food into a lump that is small enough to swallow. It then flicks the lump toward your food pipe, or **esophagus**.

8

Letting the juice loose

Tiny salivary glands are scattered all around your mouth, but most juice comes from three main pairs—located under your jaw, next to your ears, and under your tongue. Not all saliva is watery. Some glands make really gooey juice, which helps to stick bits of food together.

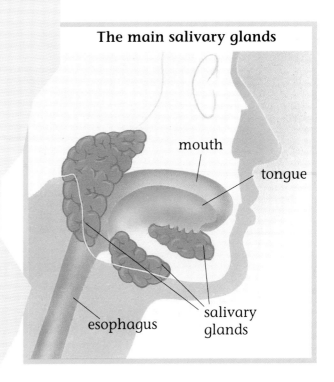

The main salivary glands

mouth

tongue

salivary glands

esophagus

soft palate closes off tunnel to nose

food goes down esophagus

Down the right way

When you are ready to swallow, two fleshy trapdoors close to stop the food from going the wrong way. One, called the **epiglottis**, stops it from falling into your **windpipe**. The other, the **soft palate**, stops it from going up your nose.

Don't talk—eat

Have you ever choked because you were eating and talking at the same time? You choke when food goes down your windpipe. Your epiglottis gets confused if you talk with your mouth full. It thinks it should cover your windpipe so you can swallow, but it also wants to stay open so you can talk.

9

PUMPING PIPE

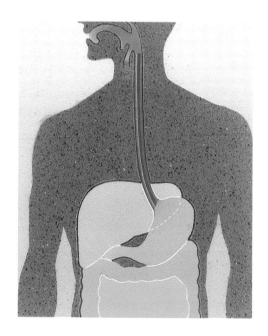

*E*very time you swallow a lump of food, a muscular pipeline called your esophagus pumps it toward your stomach.

muscles squeeze on moist lump of food

Pumping pairs

Your **esophagus** consists of two different types of muscle. Circular ones, on the inside, are ring-shaped. **Longitudinal muscles**, on the outside, are long and stringy. They all work together in a special rippling rhythm, transporting food along the pipeline.

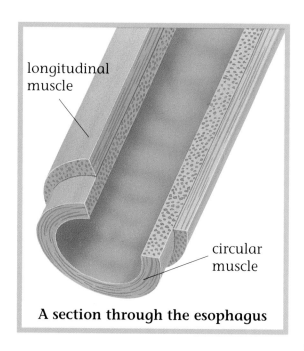

longitudinal muscle

circular muscle

A section through the esophagus

Moving along

When you swallow, muscles at the top of your esophagus tighten to trap the moist lump of food inside. As this happens, muscles further along the tube relax, letting the lump move along it a little.

Muscles keep changing like this all the way down your pumping pipe. The action, called **peristalsis**, keeps food on the move throughout most of your digestive system.

Space food

The muscles in your esophagus work so well, you can even eat when you're upside down. When astronauts are in space, there's no gravity to pull their food downward through their bodies. But they're still able to eat just as they do on Earth.

Pardon me!

You don't only swallow food when you eat. You also gulp down lots of air. Usually, this air travels harmlessly to your stomach. But if you swallow too much, you have to puff it up out of your mouth again. This is why you burp.

Down and out

The esophagus has a smooth lining that makes its own moisture. This acts like a built-in oiler, making it easier for food to slip along the tube.

When the moist food reaches the end of the esophagus, a rubbery ring loosens to let it slip out into your stomach. This ring-shaped muscle is called a **sphincter**. When you're not swallowing, the sphincter stays tightly shut to stop the moist food in your stomach from returning to your esophagus.

sphincter muscle lets food into stomach

11

MIXING TANK

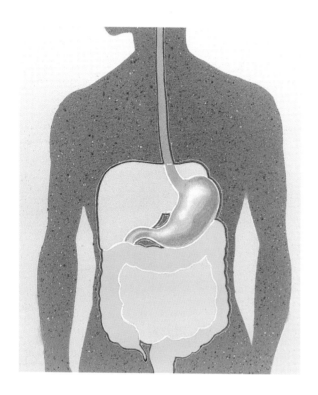

The pumping pipe leads to a wrinkly, stretchy tank that stores food and releases some of the nutrients, which are chemical substances, from it. This is your stomach.

You can usually tell when you're hungry. That's because your stomach lets you know. When it's empty, the stomach gets ready for action by producing lots of the juices it needs to work on anything inside it. As it does this, it sends messages to your brain, telling you it's time to eat. Your stomach prepares for work even if you just see, smell, or think about something tasty.

stomach lining makes juices to mix with food

Over-stuffed

*We may enjoy eating, but we can feel ill if we overdo it. An empty stomach is wrinkled like a balloon that has had all the air squeezed out of it. As it fills, these wrinkles disappear. If your stomach is stretched to its limits, it triggers **nerves** that tell your brain you're in pain. This gives you a stomach ache.*

Dinner time

Your stomach begins to produce more juices as soon as some food reaches it. These juices kill some of the germs in the food. They also start to break down the food into nutrients that your body needs.

Stomach juices are so strong, they would eat away the stomach itself if it wasn't lined with a thick, moist coating.

How does your body use the nutrients it takes from food? Find out on pages 22–25.

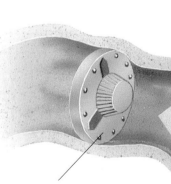

sphincter muscle opens to let food out of stomach

Churning to chyme

The walls of your stomach ripple around to mix up the food and juices inside. Gradually the contents are churned into a soupy mixture called **chyme**. Rich, fatty foods take the longest to be turned into chyme in the stomach.

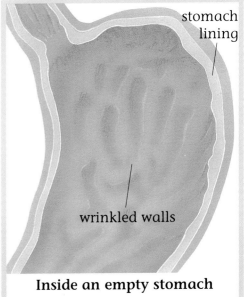

Inside an empty stomach

stomach lining

wrinkled walls

Moving on

A **sphincter** muscle at the bottom of your stomach stops the chyme from getting out. But every few minutes, it opens to let a couple of spoonfuls of chyme into your **small intestine**, the next part of your digestive system.

churning food with juices makes chyme

Saved for later

If you're very frightened, your stomach may stop sending chyme to your small intestine. That's because your body is preparing to cope with the danger at hand. It won't waste valuable **energy** on digesting food until it knows you're safe again.

ABSORBING TUBE

Chyme from the stomach passes through a 21-foot long, twisty tube called the small intestine. This absorbs most of the nutrients that the human machine needs to keep it running smoothly. It's good at mopping up because it has a fuzzy lining which helps it to absorb liquids, just like a towel.

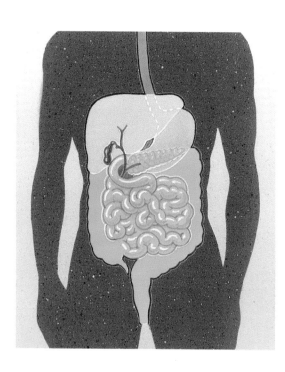

Useful juices

The action of peristalsis keeps the chyme moving along your **small intestine**, where it becomes something called chyle. As it slowly moves through the tube, the chyle mixes with more juices that help break down its ingredients into simpler substances. Some of these juices come from **glands** in the tube itself. Other juices come from an organ called the **pancreas**.

A yellowish-green liquid called **bile** also helps to break down chyle in the small intestine. It comes from a little sack called your **gallbladder**. Bile contains worn-out parts of your blood. That's what makes it yellowish-green. It's also what makes your **feces** and **urine** brown and yellow.

leaky walls let nutrients through into blood

Where is bile made? Find out on pages 18–19.

14

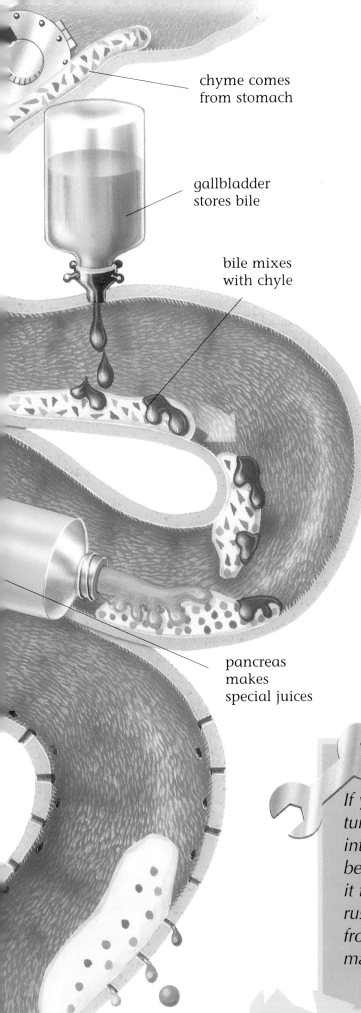

chyme comes
from stomach

gallbladder
stores bile

bile mixes
with chyle

pancreas
makes
special juices

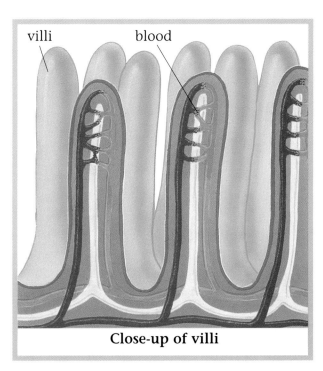

villi   blood

Close-up of villi

Mopping up

The lining of your small intestine contains millions of tiny, finger-like tufts called **villi**. These villi soak up any nutrients from the chyle passing through.

Fine tubes inside your villi pass the mopped-up nutrients into your blood, ready to be put to good use. Most of this happens in the first 10 inches of your small intestine. The rest of the pipe, over 20 feet long, is handy to deal with emergencies, like extra-large meals!

Emergency eject

If you've ever had diarrhea (a runny tummy), you've experienced your small intestine's safety system at work. If it becomes irritated, by germs for instance, it forces all its contents through in a huge rush. This prevents the germs from harming your body and makes you run to the toilet.

REJECT CHUTE

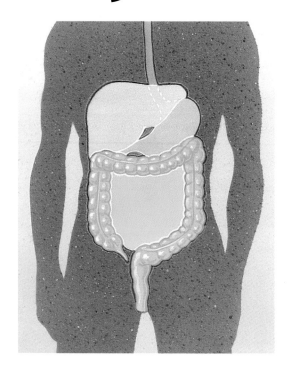

*T*he very end of the food processor is a reject chute and waste disposal system, consisting of your large intestine and rectum. This is the last stop for unwanted parts of your food.

Your large intestine—or **colon**—is a short, fat tube. It has a final chance to soak up any **vitamins** left in your chyle. It also drains out water and salt, making the chyle drier and more compact. Muscles gently shift the chyle along, breaking it up into lumps that are easy to dispose of. A moist coating helps the lumps to move along.

Generous germs

Amazingly, your colon couldn't do its work without germs. Millions of harmless **bacteria** live in the end of the tube, feeding on the remains of the chyle. As they **digest** it, they release vitamins and plenty of gas.

Out the other end

Three or four times a day, your colon pushes waste into a stretchy sack called your **rectum**. When this is full, you feel the need to go to the toilet. You don't usually have to go straight away. That's because you have a **sphincter** muscle at the end of your rectum, called your **anus**. You can control this until you're ready to squeeze out a lump of solid waste, or **feces**.

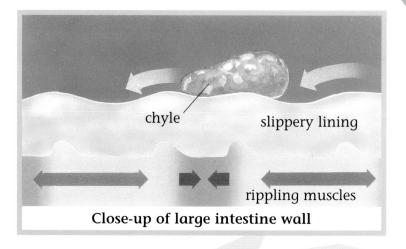

chyle

slippery lining

rippling muscles

Close-up of large intestine wall

Waste of space?

At the top of your large intestine is a tiny organ called an appendix. Some animals use their appendix to break down hard foods like twigs, but you don't need yours at all!

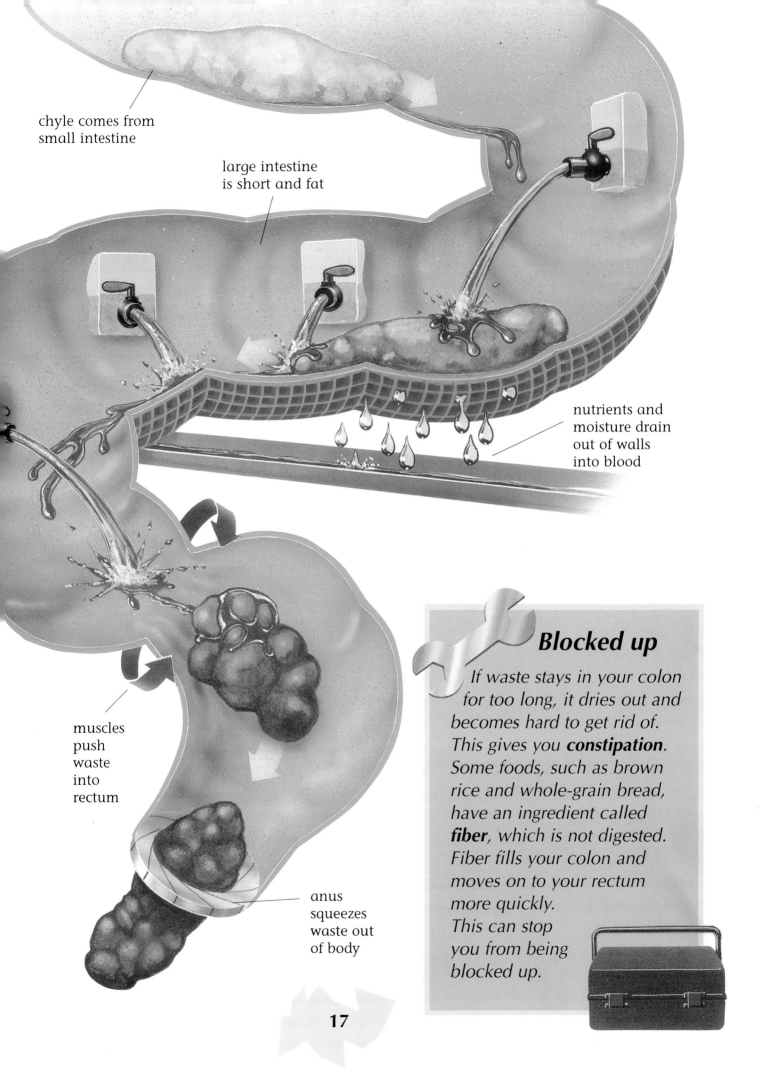

chyle comes from
small intestine

large intestine
is short and fat

nutrients and
moisture drain
out of walls
into blood

muscles
push
waste
into
rectum

anus
squeezes
waste out
of body

Blocked up

If waste stays in your colon
for too long, it dries out and
becomes hard to get rid of.
This gives you **constipation**.
Some foods, such as brown
rice and whole-grain bread,
have an ingredient called
fiber, which is not digested.
Fiber fills your colon and
moves on to your rectum
more quickly.
This can stop
you from being
blocked up.

CHEMICAL WORKS

*T*he human machine has an amazing mini-factory called the liver. It cleans, recycles, scraps, and stores, helping your body make use of the fuel it has broken down.

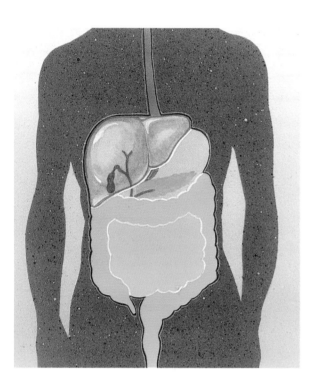

Nutrients absorbed as you **digest** are taken to your liver by your blood. Once your liver has worked on them, they are ready to help your body grow, repair itself, and stay healthy.

Restore, reject, recycle

The blood **cells** that carry nutrients around your body are constantly being worn out and replaced. When a cell needs replacing, your liver removes any useful substances, such as **iron**, and puts them back into your blood. It dumps some of the unwanted parts into a liquid it makes called **bile**, which is kept in a little sack called the **gallbladder**.

Your liver also clears away poisons. It breaks them down and sends them to your **kidneys**. Alcohol is one of the worst poisons—too much of it can ruin your liver for good.

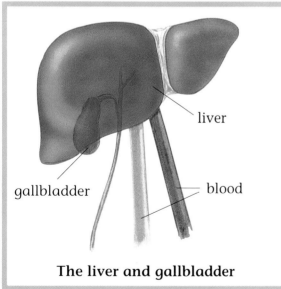

liver

gallbladder

blood

The liver and gallbladder

Where does bile go?
Why else do we need it?
Find out on pages 14–15.

Sweet supplies

Sometimes your blood absorbs more nutrients than your body needs all at once. Your liver can save them for future use. When there's too much sugar in your blood, for instance, your liver stores some of it. It puts the sugar back into your blood when you need a burst of **energy**, but if there's still too much to use, it turns it into fat.

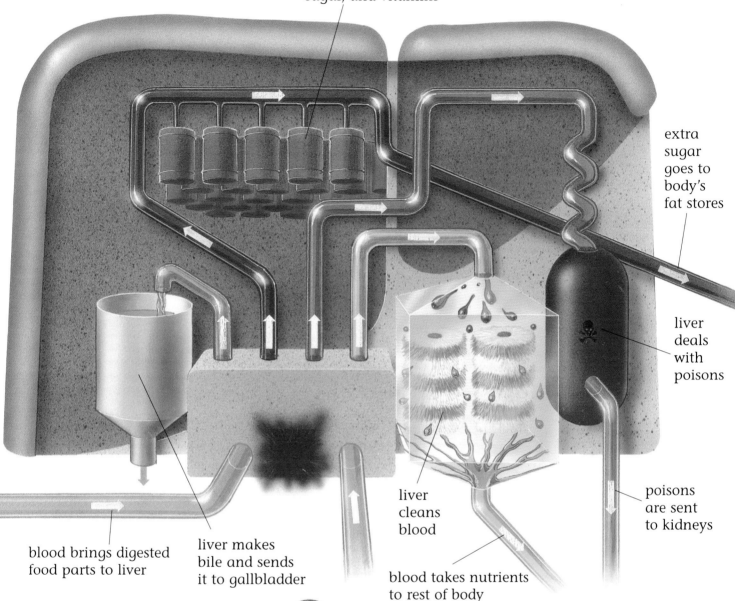

liver stores blood, sugar, and vitamins

extra sugar goes to body's fat stores

liver deals with poisons

poisons are sent to kidneys

liver cleans blood

blood takes nutrients to rest of body

liver makes bile and sends it to gallbladder

blood brings digested food parts to liver

Sugar problem

Some people have a condition called **diabetes**, *which means that their liver can't control the sugar in their blood. This is because their* **pancreas** *doesn't produce enough, if any,* **insulin.** *They must be careful about what they eat, and may have to inject insulin into their bodies.*

Built-in radiator

Did you know you had your own central heating system? As blood flows through the liver, its temperature rises. This helps to keep you warm as it travels around your body.

WATERWORKS

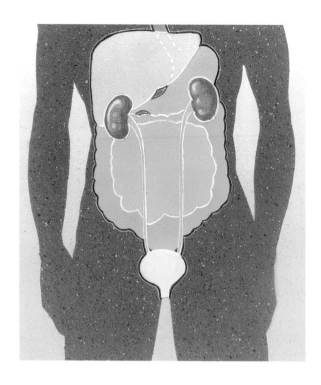

T wo special filters—your kidneys—are working all the time to make sure your blood doesn't become too salty, waterlogged, or full of minerals.

Every time you urinate, you drain some water from your body. This water contains salts, **minerals**, and some worn-out parts that your body needs to lose. These have all been sifted out by your **kidneys**.

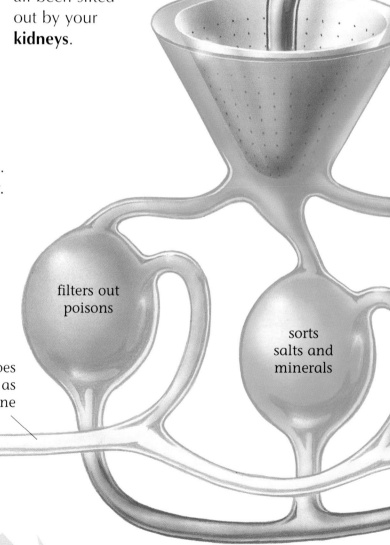

Finding the balance

You need to have just the right amount of water, salts, and minerals in your blood. Otherwise your body won't work properly.

Your kidneys are checking the levels of these substances all the time. If you have too much, they filter some out and send them to a storage tank called your **bladder**. You empty your bladder when you urinate.

filters out poisons

sorts salts and minerals

overflow goes to bladder as urine

Toxic waste

Blood goes to the kidneys after it has been to the liver. It's full of poisons and parts from your body that the liver has broken down, ready to remove. Your kidneys send these to the bladder, too.

Hot and cold

In hot weather you produce less urine than you do on cold days. That's because you lose some extra water and salt when you sweat.

How a nephron works

blood

nephron sucks some water, salts, and minerals out of blood

urine

some water and minerals move back into blood

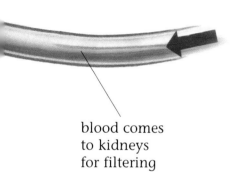

blood comes to kidneys for filtering

Super suction

Each kidney contains about a million tiny, leaky tubes, called **nephrons**. When blood enters your kidneys, it is squeezed through these nephrons at high speed.

Most blood travels all the way through the nephrons. But some of the water, salts, and minerals it contains seep out of their walls. The kidneys absorb these substances and send any unwanted amounts to the bladder as urine. The bladder can hold almost as much as two drink cans full of urine before you feel desperate to empty it.

balances water level

filtered blood goes to body

Special gift

Sometimes a person's kidneys both break down. If this happens, they may need an emergency operation called a transplant. Amazingly, someone healthy can give them one of their own good kidneys and still live normally with the one they have left.

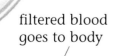

CONSTRUCTION

*T*he human machine needs food as fuel, to build its parts and to keep it in working order. You should make sure your food contains all the right things to do these jobs.

By the time you're fully grown, you'll be at least 20 times heavier than you were when you were born. All the extra bone, flesh, skin, and other body parts you grow are made up from substances that come from your food.

The parts of food that your body needs are the **nutrients**. You use them to grow, repair body parts, replace them, and keep them working. Each strand of hair, for example, is replaced with a new one every two to six years. When you cut your skin, nutrients help new **cells** grow to heal it.

If you eat a wide variety of foods, such as the ones shown in this basket, you'll probably get all the nutrients you need. It's also important to drink plenty of water. This is known as having a **balanced diet**.

Carbohydrates

These are your body's batteries. Your liver turns them into simple sugars that your cells can burn to release **energy**. Carbohydrates should be the main part of your daily diet. They mostly come from foods such as rice, bread, pasta, and potatoes. You'll find lesser amounts in fruits and vegetables.

Vitamins

Your body needs small amounts of **vitamins** to help how it works. For example, it needs vitamin C to grow healthy skin and fight diseases. You'll find vitamin C in fruits such as oranges.

22

KIT

Fantastic fiber

Some parts of your fuel give you no nutrients at all. Bulky stuff called **fiber**, found mostly in whole-grain foods and vegetables, passes all the way through your body without being digested. But you still need to eat plenty of it to keep your food processor healthy (see page 17).

Proteins

These help your body to make and repair cells. They are mainly found in meat, milk, cheese, nuts, beans, and cereals. When you're running low on carbohydrates, your body can use proteins as energy supplies.

Minerals

These are used for special tasks in the body. Your red blood cells need **iron**, for example, to carry **oxygen** around your body. Most iron is found in red meat and dark green vegetables. You need **calcium**, an ingredient in milk, cheese, and eggs, to make strong teeth and bones.

Fats and oils

These are found in foods such as butter, milk, nuts, and meat. Your body can turn them into sugar for energy. They also help you to soak up certain vitamins.

FUEL GAUGE

Just like a car or radio, the human machine needs energy to keep it going. You don't need a battery or gas—your fuel is the food you eat.

Unlike most machines, your body can't be switched off. Even when you're sitting still or sleeping, you need some **energy** just to keep your body going and to stay warm.

Everyone's energy needs are different. Children, for example, use up lots of extra energy as they grow. Energy is often measured in **kilocalories** (kcal). Most of us use between 50 and 150 kilocalories an hour, but the more active you are, the more fuel you burn.

Fuel force

Some foods give you more energy than others. That's because they contain more kilocalories. The more kilocalories you eat, the more energy you should have.

This diagram shows how long you could run for on the energy that some different foods give you. Remember though—some foods that are full of energy aren't always the best ones to eat to keep you fit, healthy, and ready for action!

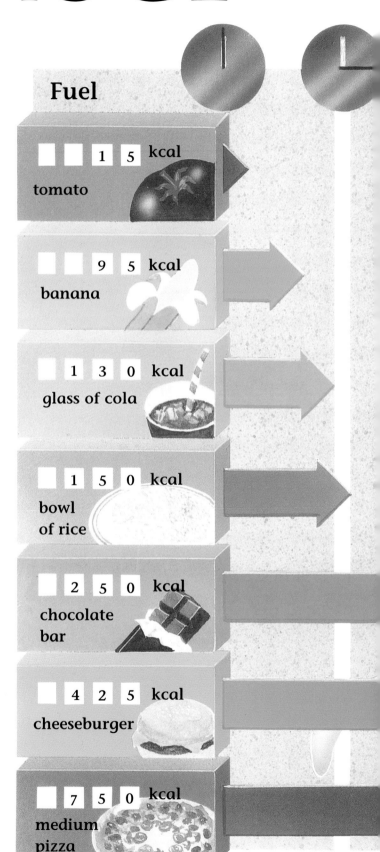

Fuel

1 5 kcal
tomato

9 5 kcal
banana

1 3 0 kcal
glass of cola

1 5 0 kcal
bowl of rice

2 5 0 kcal
chocolate bar

4 2 5 kcal
cheeseburger

7 5 0 kcal
medium pizza

Running time

What should go into your fuel? Find out on pages 22–23.

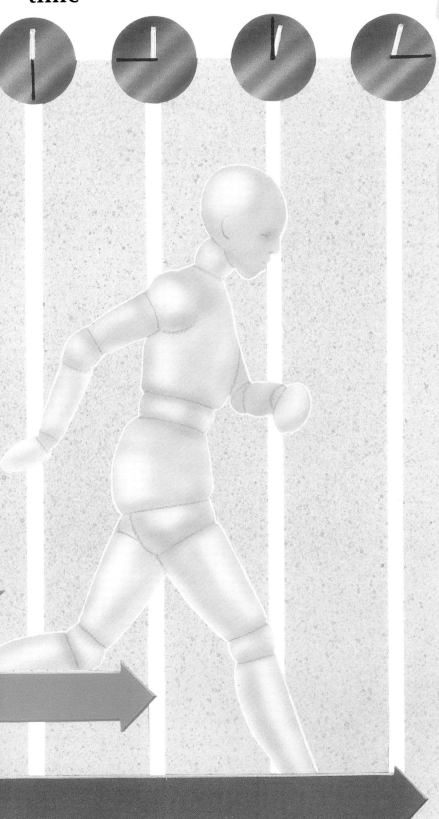

Fat faults

Some high-energy foods, such as burgers and chips, are also full of fat. If too many of the kilocalories you eat come from fat, you could harm your body and may even put a strain on your heart. But by eating a good **balanced diet**, you'll get all the energy you need, from all the right things.

Running on empty?

When your fuel gauge is low, you start to feel hungry. But you need to fill your tank with the right amounts. If you eat more than you burn, your body stores the surplus as fat. If you eat too little, it converts some of your fat into energy. If your body is very short of fuel, it may even need to burn up the proteins in your muscles.

Chill factor

Did you know that we need more energy on cold days? That's because we lose more of our body heat into the cold air around us. Thin people lose heat more quickly than people with more body fat.

CARE AND SERVICING

The human food processor needs to last for life, so it's a good idea to look after it and give it regular check-ups.

Fortunately, your digestive system carries out many of its own repairs. For instance, every few days, it completely renews the lining of the **small intestine**. But there's also plenty you can do to help your food processor to run smoothly.

Stay away from poisons

Your liver helps you to get rid of poisons, but there's only so much it can do. Drinking too much alcohol or abusing drugs can damage your liver for life.

Guard against germs

You may not be able to see them, but all around you there are germs that could harm your food processor. Always wash your hands after going to the toilet and before you eat. This will make you less likely to wipe germs onto your food.

Never eat things that haven't been stored or cooked properly—these are favorite hiding places for deadly **bacteria**.

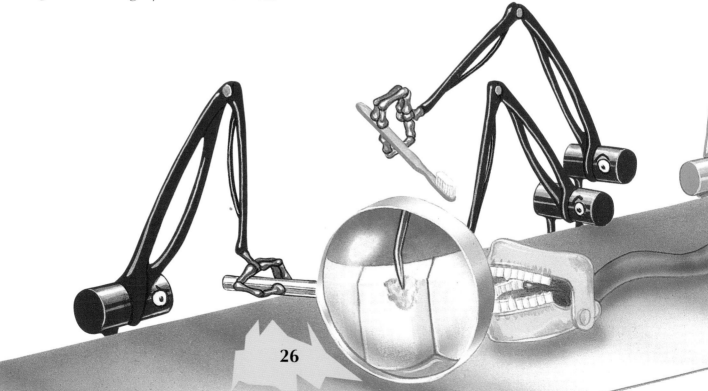

Look after your teeth

Sugary foods, such as sweets and soft drinks, feed germs that decay your teeth, so it's best not to eat them too often. Scrubbing your teeth every morning and evening helps to clear away germs and give you a shiny white smile. You also need to visit a dentist regularly, to keep your teeth healthy and to correct any problems.

Inspection

If your food processor does go wrong, the best person to see is a doctor. They'll probably start by asking what fuel you've put in—then they may examine what comes out. Doctors can tell a lot from testing your **urine** and **feces**—and even more from taking a small sample of your blood.

Built to last

If you live to a ripe old age, you can expect to eat more than 80,000 meals. Your amazing food processor works all through your life, even when you're not eating. That means it should be able to run non-stop for around 650,000 hours!

OTHER MODELS

Your digestive system is perfectly suited to the human machine. But many other animals have very different food processors. Here are just a few of the other models around.

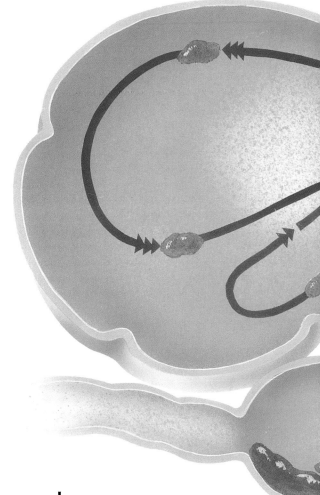

Complicated cows

We only need one simple stomach, but a cow has four. It needs them all to help break down the tough grass and hay that it feeds on.

When a cow swallows, the food travels into two stomachs, where it starts to break down. Then it comes back up into the cow's mouth as a slushy mixture called cud. The cow chews the cud before swallowing it again, so that it can pass on easily into the third stomach, and from there into the fourth. Animals that eat like this are called ruminants.

Stretchy snakes

Snakes are long and skinny, but they can eat creatures much bigger than themselves. They can't chew their food like we do. Instead, they have special jaws, which come apart and open wide enough to swallow an animal whole.

This means the rest of the snake's food processor has a lot of work to do to break down the food. Snakes may have to rest for weeks after a big meal because they're too full and tired to move.

How snakes swallow their food

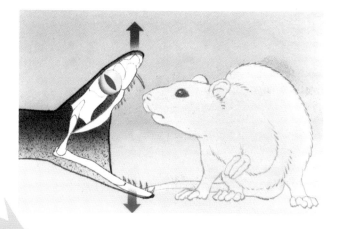

28

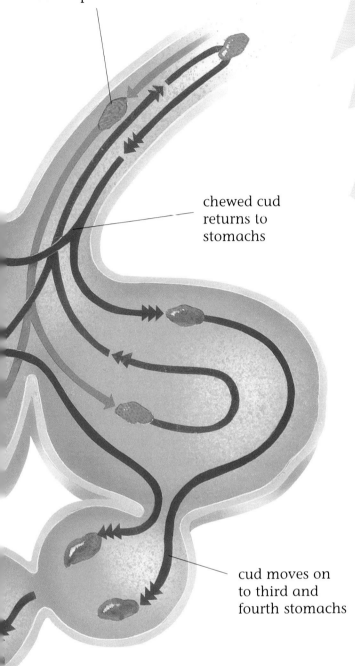

food goes into first two stomachs, then moves back up to mouth

chewed cud returns to stomachs

cud moves on to third and fourth stomachs

Bloodsuckers

Creatures such as ticks and leeches don't chew and **digest** food like we do. They feed on the blood of other animals, which is already full of nutrients. They do this by making a tiny hole in the animal's skin and sucking the blood out of it. Creatures that feed like this are known as parasites.

Tough tigers

Tigers have huge, sharp **canines** that can tear easily through raw meat. They can eat so much in one session that they don't need another meal for over a week.

Wriggly worms

The worm's digestive system runs through its entire body. This creature burrows through its food, eats it, then leaves a trail of leftovers called a worm cast.

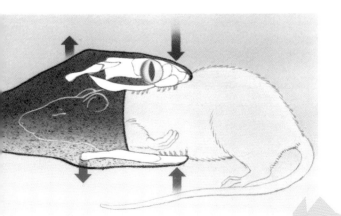

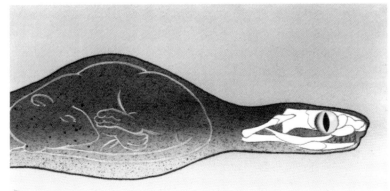

GLOSSARY

anus The ring-shaped muscle at the end of your digestive system.

bacteria Types of germs—tiny living things made of just one cell.

balanced diet A variety of foods that contain all the nutrients you need.

bile A yellowish-green liquid made by the liver that helps break down fats in the small intestine.

bladder A sack that stores urine made by the kidneys. You empty it when urinating.

calcium The mineral that your bones are made of. Dairy products, eggs, fish, and soybeans are good sources of calcium.

canines Sharp, pointed side teeth that are used to rip food into smaller pieces.

cells The billions of very tiny parts that combine to make various tissues in your body.

chyme The soupy mixture made when food is broken down by juices in the stomach.

colon Another name for the large intestine, the short, fat tube near the end of your digestive system.

constipation Having difficulty passing feces because they are dry and hard.

dentine The bone-like layer of your teeth, underneath the enamel.

diabetes The disease people have when their pancreas can't make enough, if any, insulin. The sugar level in their blood can rise dramatically, making them ill.

digest To break down food so that it can be absorbed by the body.

enamel The hard, pearly white outer layer that covers and protects your teeth.

energy The store of power that you need for your body to do anything at all.

epiglottis The fleshy trapdoor that can close over the opening to your windpipe.

esophagus The food pipe that connects your mouth to your stomach.

feces Excrement or waste matter.

fiber A bulky material that your body can't digest.

gallbladder A tiny sack, linked to the liver, that stores bile.

glands Parts of the body that make juices.

incisors The spade-shaped front teeth.

insulin A chemical produced by the pancreas. The liver needs insulin to control the levels of sugar in the blood.

iron An important mineral, found mainly in red meat and leafy green vegetables.

kidneys The pair of organs that separate water and waste from blood and excrete them as urine.

kilocalorie A measure of the energy you can get from food.

longitudinal muscles Muscles that lie lengthways along a digestive tube.

minerals Chemicals, such as calcium and iron, that your body uses to form body parts like bone and blood cells.

molars The wide, flat back teeth that can grind up food.

nephrons Tiny tubes in your kidneys that filter out unwanted water, salts, and minerals.

nerves Fine threads that carry messages between your brain and other body parts.

nutrients The chemical substances in food that your body needs to survive.

oxygen A gas that is found in air. It enters your body when you breathe. Your body needs it for your cells to work properly.

pancreas An organ that makes digestive juices and chemicals such as insulin.

peristalsis The rippling muscle action that pushes food along your digestive tubes.

rectum A stretchy sack at the end of the colon that holds waste.

saliva The juice in your mouth that softens your food, starts to break down nutrients in it, and binds the pieces together.

small intestine The long, twisty tube that connects your stomach to your colon. This is where most of the nutrients in your food are absorbed.

soft palate A fleshy trapdoor that can cover the tube connecting your mouth to your nose.

sphincter A ring-shaped muscle that can tighten to close off a pipe or relax to open it and let things through.

urine A liquid produced in your kidneys and stored in your bladder.

villi The tiny, finger-like tufts that line the small intestine and absorb nutrients.

vitamins Chemicals in food that your body needs to help the way it works.

windpipe The tube that air passes through when you breathe. It leads from your throat to your lungs.

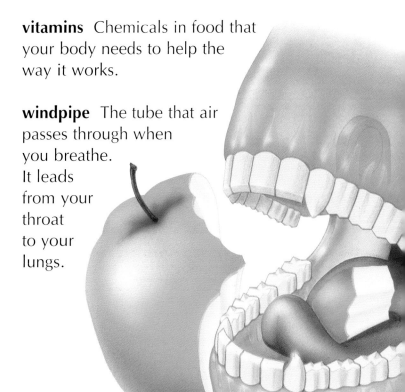

INDEX